# PARADE OF GHOSTS

### Roger Hecht

# PARADE OF GHOSTS

## Roger Hecht

A POEM IN SEQUENCE FORM

**THE LIGHTNING TREE** — Jene Lyon, Publisher
Post Office Box 1837    Santa Fé, New Mexico 87501    U.S.A.

Parts of PARADE OF GHOSTS appeared in: *Audience, Kumanitu, The Minnesota Review, New World Writing, Quarterly Review of Literature, The Sewanee Review* and *Voyages*. Certain parts of this book have been reprinted from books © 1966 and 1970 by Roger Hecht, with permission of The Swallow Press, Inc.

Library of Congress Catalog Card Number: 75-46071

ISBN: 0-89016-017-1   Paper

ISBN: 0-89016-018-X   Cloth

Printed in the United States of America

THE LIGHTNING TREE — JENE LYON, PUBLISHER

P. O. Box 1837   Santa Fé, New Mexico 87501   U.S.A.

"Let us hope that Fable may, in what shall follow, so submit
to the purifying processes of Reason as to take the character
of exact history."

—Plutarch, Theseus

"...They were intelligent, but what paths would their in-
telligence select? They were quick, but what solution of in-
soluble problems would quickness hurry? They were scientif-
ic, and what control would their science exercise over their
destiny? They were mild, but what corruptions would their
relaxations bring? They were peaceful, but by what machin-
ery were their corruptions to be purged? What object, be-
sides physical content, must a democratic continent aspire
to attain?..."

—Henry Adams on American Character in 1815 in<br>History of the United States During the<br>Administration of James Madison

For Joe, Bill, Jane, Fred, Carol, Allen, Linda, Eva, Ted and Jim

# CONTENTS

# I

## ALVAR NUÑEZ CABEZA DE VACA

(Cabeza de Vaca supposedly died in Spain in 1557. However, there is no proof of his death. He had been jailed for describing in his *Narrative* the miracles his companions and he performed. And for that reason no death certificate in his name was ever issued by the priests who, I gather, issued such certificates for the purpose of permitting the dead to be buried in sacred ground. Thus, while it's probable that de Vaca died in Spain in 1557, by empirical standards we do not know that he died then, there, or at any other time in any place. The unsettled controversy over the truth and/or falsity of the *Narrative* lasted about one century. I have taken as truth de Vaca's account. The "Seven Cities" mentioned are the Seven Cities of Cibola which have never been found.)

Cabeza de Vaca, Head of a Cow, dead or not dead,
Hidden somewhere in the crooked arm of Spain,
A voyager by choice in search of gold
And the Seven Cities that were supposed to lead
Directly into China—what will remain
Of your long sojourn on this savage coast?
Men know your story, and the story's old
Enough to leave you unremembered, nameless, lost
In the parade of places, names and dates
That is for us our history. History is facts.

These facts are known: in 1528,
Thinking you were somewhere in New Spain
(Which now is Mexico), six hundred men
Landed near Tampa Bay. By fever and combat
With hostile Indians your company was drained;
And when you floated past the Mississippi's mouth
And landed not far from what's now Galveston,
How few of you had not been caught by death!
Four of you if I number as a man
The slave you did not count or count upon.

You languished on that island in the sun,
The wet, the wind, and took what the earth provides—
Nuts, berries, roots—for your rich sustenance.
Years, years. The rest is miracle:
One of them was the clean removal of an arrowhead
From the heart of an Indian with a knife's blade.
The man lived. You knew no medicine nor other instruments
Than those God gave to man for good and ill,
Than those He still gives to the mind and flesh and brief
Rage of the spirit. You tried your own belief

By converting Indians to our strange Lord,
And that mainly done by the savage black
The Indians worshipped, followed as a god,
And served and saved that he might save their hard
And brittle pastures for their children's sake.
Was Texas saved? In 1536,
Led by those hordes of Indians and salt-sore, nearly dead,
You wandered into Spanish guards. These are the facts:

The Indians were slaughtered in the name
Of God and the Captain and the King of Spain.

More than three centuries ago you returned to Spain
And later died or did not die—nobody knows
The truth and there are few who care to search for it
For its own sake.
And you may wander in the legion of the lost—
Head or Skull of a Cow and not much more
Of your ruining flesh can possibly remain—
Another century or more without a rest
Before the bishops confer on you a fate;
They are too taxed to argue even now.
And I, who found your *Narrative* in an abandoned book,
Ask: why have you lived? What have you suffered for?

Cabeza de Vaca, Head of a Cow, dead or not dead,
What if anything do these facts mean?
Is history a row of accidents?
Are men the blind performers of the blood?
Do we have any choice to stop, begin,
Stand still, at least in part to forge our fate?
Or do we float, vessels of chance, mischance,
As on calm water nowhere? In mixed shade and light
Do we tell ourselves we approach the longed-for coast
Of promised Eden? . . .It is the past
That's present makes each one of us, like you, a ghost
Not known, not mourned, not damned, not blessed, not dead.

**II**

## A WORK OF DARKNESS

(Shortly before her execution, the washerwoman **Goody** Glover, in Boston Prison, 1688, addresses her God.)

Consider, Sir, I have no children, none.
My worldly goods, these ragged clothes, that house
And what it holds, all this my wretchedness,
And my poor babies, puppets, made of rags.
Nothing else. Consider, I am old.

What is my story?
When they came, the Goodwin children, I
Would lick my fingers, stroke these rags, my only **dears.**
The living children then would seem to sleep
Or flail their arms or fly across the room
Or they would howl and roll. Strange, very strange.
And yet more strange, the children would return
And I would stroke my dolls, and the events
That happened once would so recur it seemed
There was no way of telling if they played
As children play or if they took the burden
Of feigning life for my poor lifeless babies.
What's the harm of love? I meant love,
And love the children gave me, all the children,
Although I have no children, no, none, none.

Tomorrow or today, Sir, I must die
For having been most solemnly declared

By gentlemen, these several judges, evil,
Nothing but a witch.
Deliver me from prison, Sir, I beg you,
And burn me for the woman that I am
But not the fiend others pretend I am.

What is the truth?
We are in your hands and you must judge.

### III

## SONNET

When Cotton Mather looked for Paradise,
He stood beside the damp and open graves
Of children who had lost their lives through fear
Or in some agony he could not trace.
To Mather absolution seemed so near
It hid behind the muscles of the face
Of one poor child with Satan in her hair.
"Is death alive and ranging everywhere,"
He asked in his lament. But in the park,
Where yesterday I went to note the leaves,
I saw two children carving on a bark
Their small initials; and I thought that this
Was their one permanence, their single mark
Against the sun that rolls from dark to dark.

# IV

## JEFFERSON TO JEFFERSON

### (1801)

Mr. Hamilton propositioned me.
I thanked him. I accepted. I became
Third President by bribe and one small crime,
Political treachery.
What men will do when wound in power's dream
And chasing the blown bubble, fame,
I seem to see as I mount destiny
And canter down the road to what will be
America, the long sought, new found Rome.

# V

## AARON BURR (1756-1836)

### I

Jonquil dead; and when no aster stalk
Reminded you of dahlia or late rows
Of harvesting,
   You hid yourself in priestly cloak
To get a message past St. Lawrence floes,
To Montgomery, dead already in attack.
A man in passion rides a savage horse.
Still, grey the wing, or brown the wing,
      birdthroat,
Against the maple or the evergreen.
   With Arnold full of drink and wind
Shot in the leg, wrathbound,
With storm of season, eating nut and root,
One army cut in two,
What could the pock-faced Washington anticipate
If not a wreck?
More than the wounded died in the snow
At Montreal, and at Quebec.
   Birdthroat
Swells to its ordinary offer and small sound
Against the evergreen.
   Rebuke:
Your passage to obscurity.
Buff and white the throat, keening clarity
Late or soon,
  In the night.

## II

You followed darkness like a dream:
T. Paine at the drumhead instead of table;
Yourself commander at the 'Gulf': a scene of ice,
And the stars frozen to tearblaze overhead.
The men were scurvy-thin and scratching lice.
Steuben, with an aide, inducing men
To exercise:
To form, reform, and, once more, form a line.
Washington clamped wooden teeth, untalkable.
Hamilton felt sure Spring would arrive.
       Which got a laugh.
Dark on the ice: across the Delaware
Some German troops made noisy jubilee.
       The chance.
While Germans drank and formed themselves for
             dance,
The ragged chaff
Took Durhams oared by men from Marblehead,
Left boards with blood; and, in the Winter air,
Walked into Trenton to join the play
The morning after Christmas day:
       'The world turned upside down.'
Hamilton sent a cannonball
Into your father's hall
At Princeton in a scene of ice.
When men wrapped cloth about their feet
To slow the ooze of blood, when scurvyscourge
Made Hell a tent at Valley Forge,
When Spring did come, shad tasted sweet.

## III

You followed darkness down into the night
        Where grey, where brown,
Where black, cream-white,
        And slight for less than one foot long,
Drums, late or soon,
        In the night, before the day,
The whippoorwill with strident song.


A bullet or a ball for Hamilton;
He had, in the concern of corporate finance,
Offered an old man a crown.
        In the dance
Of Democratic manners still the tune:
        "Give us more money; God bless us all."
And you, the almost founder of Tammany Hall,
Turned, turned at last,
        South, southwest:
Acquitted twice of a conspiracy
To overthrow America, from plain to plain,
Where souls are sales, with brawn for brain,
And burying the yellow grain
        In old vacuity.
When will the whippoorwill call
        With majesty
From bough of oak or evergreen
In grey, in brown, in black, in white,
Clear, clear, clear,
In the foliage of night,
To lovers as they pass?

When will the whippoorwill call
From a bough where Spanish moss
Tightens in the starsprayed air
As lovers issue down the passages of light
That still remain?
When will the whippoorwill call?
After the day and in the night.

# VI

## WESTWARD

### I

They were not many. And they must have been
Sick, weary, sore, confused and nearly set
To give it up as an outrageous plan.
But then there came the smell of something wet
Like mist, like rain, like salt. And that was new.
One of the few, the Captain, sat and wrote:
*"Ocian in view. O! the joy."*
That winter they remained, then started on
The long return to Mr. Jefferson
With word about the strangeness they had seen,
Strangeness that left them never quite the same.
And yet before another year was through,
John Astor started shipping his hides home
East around the Cape. Westering began,
Reviving El Dorado. Where was that?
Fur trapping started and the race was on
To seize the old dream some men still pursue.

### II

I thought I saw them move again before me,
Settlers, soldiers, squatters, tagalongs,
Fur trappers and the men who poled pirogues
With and against the current. All of them
Moving, always moving,
And dreaming forward west, west, further west.

In leather, beaver clothes,
Primed flintlocks riding on their laps, they sang
To keep their courage high a slaw of songs
And whistled hymns while plunging zigzag through
Blackfoot country tall with buffalo grass
Until they vanished at a portage crossroads
Where history, oblivion and myth
Exactly intersect in dust.
                    I stared.
I coughed. I rubbed my eyes. But I could see
A quarreling of dust for signature
As if no names were notched and none had been.
That absence is their only x-mark left.

# VII

## SOLDIER'S STORY

I recall
Snow like no other snow,
Mud to the knees,
The march from where to where.
And rain. And stench. And wind.
A few of us would fall,
A few would kneel to rest—
Casualties.
What was left stayed to drag
Comrades and horses west
To France, wherever that was
Beyond the storm-hemisphere.
The midnight I reached home
And since then I recall
No other soldier's name,
No other soldier's face,
Only Napoleon.
I recall
A badge, a cap, a flag,
Fingers, part of a leg,
Shreds of the things that were men
Planted in the snow,
Signposts for the damned
As long as such signs last.
Tomorrow, Waterloo.
And after death, another war?

# VIII

## A NOTE FROM SENATOR WEBSTER

The sum you mention, Sir, is far too low
For me to render services you need.
If you can up the ante, I'll bestow
Great blessings on your good work and my greed.
The Bible says, brethren, what shall we do?
Please think on that and answer with Godspeed.

# IX

## FROM DONNER PASS

Never the very worst
Had I undergone,
Never had I been first
To do what I had done
Until I came to this
Wilderness of snow
Where all of us went lost.
For twenty-five days
I have eaten the flesh
And marrow of my wife
And only son
As all the others have done.
I have eaten three others, too.
Now they are gone.
What can I do?
How can I live?
How little of us remains!
Some clothes. Some skulls. Some bones.
Some scraps of men.
I have nothing to chew,
Nothing but snow
And what is left of me.
That is not enough.
Nothing is.

# X

## FRANCIS PARKMAN (1823-1893)

'The last stages of an infirm life are filthy roads. I find the further one goes from the capital, the more tedious the miles grow, and the more rough and disagreeable the way.'
—Lord Harvey to Lady Mary Wortley Montague

### I

Shall I have time, below a cherry bough,
After blossoms blight, as the lovers twine,
To come, to pluck a berry, and to eat?
   Summer shall green the grass
Before, as sure as fire of the leaf,
   I may see ripening fruit
Streaked with dewshine.
   The sun shall burn a row
Of browning grass
Where I will stand and notch a cherry bough
With your initials, as a lover might,
If there is time enough.
   No matter now.
No matter was the season of your loss
When you kept steady to your purpose
And went West
To learn the country you would write about.
Locked in your doubt,
Severe as frozen river before Spring,
Bold with your failing strength you would invest

Each crag and turn with your imagining:
America would trample underfoot
The bisoned prairies, Indians, and mine
The greening soil that you could celebrate.
Parkman, if there is time, and time enough,
I will gather cherries in the Fall,
And settle on the grass below a bough,
And eat till my hands bleed at the sunfall.

## II

Then, in the Job-long years of your distress,
Rome passed, and America like a star
Pinwheeling in the spray of morning light,
You found the rigor of your innocence
In shuffling off the Byron, Cooper, Scott.
Hand in a cage,
The fume-light steaming late into the night,
Your mind awakened to another war:
The first of seven volumes.
          But repose
Comes after certainty:
          the tribal dance,
The slicing arrows and the breast plates rage
In fury through the years of your distress
Till you made sail for Paris
          and reprieve.
The doctor said: "A fuzziness of brain;
An aggravation to the nerves; nothing more."
Except the eyes would stream and stare, beyond your leave,
At fluttering dogwood, falling to the grass.
On Boston Common, brought by intense

Constrictions, you could watch the workless men
Slide from police by body's ample sense
Of supple motion you once knew.
But still, the night work, and the trying for
A restoration, by a full response,
Of dusty lives and deeds. As morning grew
A rose came petal-wide, red with your love.

### III

Reprieve? A lily bears your name: memorial.
Far from the capital, you found the last
Stages of an infirm life are filthy roads.
So, fearing death, hand gripped the wire cage
To hold a pen upright as long as possible.
But to imagination, by consent,
America came boiling bright and fast
As any river spilling overfull:
       native gauds,
Gods, dress and speech could help fulfill
Your measure of intent.
       No matter now.
Yours was a turbulence you had to wage
Against complacency.
       Your world seemed still
A prison, Parkman, as you walked out to inhale.
Though, in your classroom, you could speak of dogwood buds,
At sixty-eight, spur horse and ride,
The capital seemed far, the prospect wide.
       Where was it now?

Well, it is Spring; and from a sandy hill

In Martins Ferry I can see where men
Once mined the land they cannot ruin now.
But, as these birds and wet leaves shall allow
Blood-cherries, in the Fall,
I will return, I will return again,
To knife your own initials in a bough
Since you have time, and I have time enough.

# XI

## FATHER AND SON

THE FATHER:  When we went West we went for gold
And more dominion. The wide land held
Its body forth in perfect pride
Of bison, pony, bear, snake, bird,

Indian, fruit and the yawning stream.
The promised land? Or Adam's dream?
Or was this savage lavishness
A foretaste of God's Paradise?

We found some gold. We killed with it
Since there's a lust or appetite
That is not fed by the yield of land
Or love—the hunger for command

That is not ever gratified.
For that we wrestled until we died
Felling the country half by half
In preparation for the grave.

THE SON:  We with your legacy travelled East
To purchase the appointed taste—
Tapestries, tables, books, beds, knives,
Teachers and manners for our lives—

To house the desert and populate
The last romance of man's estate.

For certainty that money would come
To fulfill our design, we halved our homes

And auctioned what we had to sell.
We planned and built a state of soul:
Trees and wide lawns now decorate
The graveyard guarded by a gate.

# XII

## REMEMBERING

### I

"A slight rain slowly gathering to storm;
Pushing at a cart wheel caught in mud,
A man in a Confederate uniform;
And in the cart meal sacks, a sword, piled wood,
The woman and two children looking blank
At yellow and black sky, a patch of trees.
Nobody had to tell me that they stank
And could stand soap, drying, singing, peas.
Where were they headed? West. Where they had been
There was a chimney left. They'd found the horse
Pulling the cart tied to a wooden stake
Planted smackdab where the house once was.
Next to the stake a Union boy, long dead,
Lay snug in weeds, wild flowers, waving grass,
His cocked gun pointed, spiderstringed, rust red,
His eyes fixed on a charred wedge of a plank
They reckoned Sherman set there as his sign—
A burned half of a cross.
I did what any boy would do. Of course,
Later, I had to wonder what mistake
Had driven them so far with one old horse,
No rifle and no money and no plan
Except to make a start or start again
In some wild place where they had never been.
Yes. In Missouri. No. I don't know when.
But that is how it was once there was peace.

It was in peace that empire began.
You should have heard us singing miles off tune."

II

My grandfather told me: "Only a man
Sort of seated on a plain plank sidewalk,
His back against a house, and his stump leg
Raised like a salute. Stuck against one thigh,
A bottle he would take a swig from or
He'd shelter at one thigh next to his crutch.
He was in uniform without a badge,
A stripe, a medal. I heard him once
Whistle a single snatch of 'Gary Owen.'
Each now and then I seem
To see him tipping that black Federal cap
Before the arm slides slack beside the crutch.
I know I stared at him as if by staring
I could understand
Something about that man, about that war.
But all I learned was that raised stump, that sign
That he had been defeated and survived
Even defeat to try to hand down something
To me and many other children
Who passed him staring, staring, each school day
Until that day he wasn't there.
For years I wondered if he was a dream
Until one night in sleep I saw that stump
Saluting me and saw him once more wink.
And woke remembering the way you will
Wake and remember little things, this world,
You'll want to unremember and you won't."

# XIII

## FROM ALICE JAMES' JOURNAL

### (London   1890)

A hypodermic syringe and one choice:
Either endure cancer or else, in pain,
By no more than an overdose
End all that can't be started once again.
How much I hesitate at the drugged edge
Of choice and consciousness,
Having been granted the exquisite privilege
Of knowing I have nothing else to choose
And nearly nothing left to choose between!

# XIV

## A CIRCUIT JUDGE

### (A western state in 1912)

It isn't always easy, I suppose,
But, yes, I've sentenced men to hang and then
Eaten my lunch and eaten heartily.
No trouble with digestion. No complaints.
And, thank God, no appeals. I know the law.
There's law, there's justice, and there's politics,
Sometimes perceptible, more often not,
In nearly every case. You do your best,
The very best you can do all the while
You know your very best is not enough,
Law being law, you being you, the Lord
Knows how much there is between the law's ideal,
Certainty,
And what you do and what you don't get done.
Doubts in bunches seem to crowd your conscience,
But still you have to eat, and so you do. . .
You say you're a reporter from the East,
Crammed with questions. Fire away, young man.
But when you write what you do write, you'd best
First show me what you've done so that I don't
Put my career or life in jeopardy.
You understand?
       How did I begin?
My father bought himself a colonelcy
In the Federal Army. What he aimed

To do was win himself political
Appointment by no more than bravery.
Plain foolishness. At Kenesaw, I think,
Or at Pineville, a ball removed one leg.
Then there he was, at thirty-five, discharged
With many medals, yes, with crutches, too,
And hardly in the running, you might say,
For anything substantial, being useless.
After years of water boards and such
Minor employments, he abandoned hope
The middle of one morning. Just like that.
And then he took to drink and I took off.
. . .What about my mother? Truth is, she left
Him and me together just like that,
Or so he said the one time that he spoke
Drunkenly about her. No. No marriage.
It may be that she couldn't bear the nights,
My father having been the sort of man
Who talks and talks the nonsense of his dreams.
But it still seems more likely she could not
Keep up with him in drinking. So she quit.
                Where in blazes was I?
Did I say I took off? Yes. I came West
To put as many miles between us two
As anybody could. I was a boy
Except in years. I became a tipstaff
And studied law at night the way you might,
I guess, devote yourself to pretty girls.
Perhaps I should have done a bit of that
Simply to train myself. I studied law
And then more law. It wasn't really hard,

Traveling the circuit, scrutinizing
The ways of prosecutors and the ways
Of getting someone freed. (Mainly money,
But by the book each while.) Then, too, I watched
The ways of our three judges. I soon learned
Folks don't care a hoot in hell for justice
So long as they get, when they come to court,
A great big show of legal fireworks
That somehow manages to kill the time
And some men, too, amusingly enough.
Not cynical at all. A cynic's one
Who wakes to find no toys will fall from heaven
And there he is, trapped in life. You, I, know,
Differently no doubt, we have to try
Somehow to make the world work, even if
One part of trying is a known pretending—
Not so much for ourselves, although we matter,
We tell ourselves—as for those few we love.
And no one promised any one of us
A diamond every Sunday all life long.
So anger's not called for.
                    Damn relevance
Outside of court! . . .I got my law degree
By mail. I got my job, my first real job,
Assistant State Attorney, by no more
Than paying small attentions to the child,
A wispy little thing, of the chief judge.
When she got engaged, she was so solemn
In telling me, I simply bowed my head
And blushed like dawn. I must have seemed a fool,
Standing there like that and saying nothing.

I think, but I'm not sure, she squeezed my hand
And left. When I could bear to lift my head,
I think I saw her but I can't be sure,
My eyes so blurred with tears. I know I swore
I'd never let another girl do that,
Get that far into me. So much for oaths. . .
About that time the tedium begins:
Deferment and deferment and deferment
And little enough to keep my hoping high.
I had a private practise, nothing much.
I had a wife and children, nothing much.
You know the way a life slips by. Well, sir,
One morning I was eating breakfast and
Doing my best to not look at my wife
The way she looks before noon, understand,
When someone doesn't knock but slams the door
As if that door were John L. Sullivan.
My three fried eggs and ham go skittering
Along with Junior's—he's our second son—
Whop on the floor. May screams. The fists again.
And then Priscilla—she's our middle girl—
Opens the door and in this young whelp trips,
Talking as he falls. I help him up.
Prissy pours him coffee and he says,
Half-sloshing coffee, that the judge is dead
And—would you mind giving me another cup,
I'd be obliged—you see, in this man's room
With this man's wife there with him, naked, too.
I clear my throat. I send the children out.
And then I get the youngster to repeat
What he has said and what he hasn't said.

It came as quite a shock. I was a judge
By nothing more than accident and by
A misdirected passion, both at once.
Now any man, I tell you, any man
Wants his advancement earned by his own work
And the merit of that work and nothing else.
(On some occasions you must give away
A pearl worth more than all your tribe to be
Simply recognized, indifference being
A law not written but a law no less.)
Anyway, when my black robe arrived
Finally from Chicago, it could fit
At least four men and me. But when it came,
I went to court for the first time. I swore—
When I was young, I did a lot of that—
I'd make that blasted robe exactly fit.
I knew the Latin phraseology
Backwards and forwards, and the precedents
Had been there in my mind so long it seemed
Almost as if I could, given the chance,
Speak for the prosecutor and defense
And carry on as judge without a hitch.
I started by dismissing all the charges
Lodged against the citizen who shot
That silly judge. Defense of property.
Besides, the Bible says a man must not
Covet his neighbor's land or wife or kine.
What that judge had done was clearly more
Than covet. He had taken. He had paid
The price then usual though, maybe, you
Today might think the cost, well, slightly steep.

But I can guarantee you that case made
Grand fireworks. It may be—and who knows?—
That that one case, more than my later thousands,
Made me chief judge.
                    What advice would I give?
It wouldn't matter, one way or another,
What tiny wisdoms I might offer if
I were fool enough to offer any.
When I was young, I told my children what
I believed they should have done. I think,
But I can't prove, they listened to me or
Indulgently pretended to. They did
Exactly what they wished. That led to trouble,
One trouble to the next until there was
Not one way out for them and not one way
The law could help or I could more than offer
An old man's comfort, chiefly plain palaver,
A hug, a little cash, all nothing much.
If asked for wisdom, I would shut my mouth
And try to stop what I can't help, the tears,
The phlegm that come and overcome a man,
An old man you would call a hanging judge.

# XV

## HENRY ADAMS (1838-1918)

A vacuum, your soul.
You noted nothing amiss,
And you went forth, the fool
Of all your enterprise.

Power was what you sought,
The power of the State.
Power consumed your thought
And life received your hate.

You never came to rule:
Hate begot fear. Time wound
The absence in your soul
Throughout your coil of mind

Until you could not move
Your thought. Then hatred gripped
What there was left of life:
All that you were you stopped.

Adams, your epitaph
Is locked in your fixed glare
At the absence everywhere
In a life you would not live

Of a simple thing, of hope.
Yet few men have the luck

And the greatness to escape
The lifelong hell they make
And the final Hell they seek
By no more than a book.

# XVI

## T.R.

We bought that transient Caesar fair and square.
The bastard would not stay bought. So he got
Exactly what he wanted, which was war,
And in that war two of our sons were shot.
Then he came crying to us for more, more,
Always much more to glut his appetite
And yield him what he thought was his just share
Of what was not his but our empire.
One of us said, but which one I forget,
"You're not a President. You are a whore
Not one of us has got the money for.
And there are many waiting, some quite near,
The way you did when you were lovelier."
Waving his San Juan sword, he chased us out
And then repeated, like a clown's encore,
The stunt performed for some photographer
In Eighteen Ninety-Eight: a bully fight
With nobody since nobody was there
To play war with that grinning idiot.
We felt constrained to pay his graft elsewhere.
So he became the righteous warrior
Who would have brought the money lenders' rout
With threats, nothing but words that altered—what?
Ah, now that he's the sage of Sagamore,
How many thousands go to hear him shout
Rages of words he can contain no more
Than a brute sea that lashes a mute shore?

# XVII

## WAR MEMENTO

(Somewhere in France   1915)

A boy with yellow hair, his clothes in place,
Lies stretched on mud, his strange face to the sun.
Behind him, one stripped tree, a small shell hole
More than a yard wide, one wall of a house.
And looking at the boy, a standing man
With perfect blankness set on both his eyes.
The rifle in his hands looks fresh with oil.
He stands. He stares. Nothing, nothing at all
Changes or moves. Such is the photograph
Of something ordinary in a war.
What here is awry? Plain humanity
Should have blanketed the corpse. Now the laugh
That slits his face seems a disturbing glare
Or filthy joke the dead boy settled for
The moment when he had to take the death
That mocks by laughter all eternity.
I stare, unable to salute farewell
Or give this dying any epitaph.

Something is cockeyed in that death-made grin,
Suggesting, as it does, nearly a grace
Or, maybe, a bravado out of place
With all the mud soldiers must quarter in.
But maybe that's the finest way to die
When what you know is that you have no choice

Except to carry on and carry on.
And so you smile, you smile beyond all pain.
Not consciously. But you smile nonetheless.
Forever. In a snapshot. To no one.

# XVIII

## THE LAST CRUSADE

"The Armistice was signed this morning. Everything for which
America fought has been accomplished."
—Woodrow Wilson: November 11, 1918

Black morning coat, black vest,
Striped trousers, starch-white shirt,
Over black shoes, gray spats,
Black silk tie, gold stick-pin,
Black silk opera hat
Fit the marble man
Who on the last crusade
To the old East
Split Europe as by lot
And bequeathed the divided dirt
To what was left of man
After the four-year's war
This elected, Puritan knight
Had never bargained for.
In truth and photograph he stands
At the bridge of the "George Washington,"
His eyes almost shut by sun's glaze,
Searching the fogged Atlantic for the coast
                              of France.

"Tell me what is right and I will fight for it."
Under the clutter of flags the steadfast crowds
Of faces at the cemetery gates.

Inside the gates, inside the picket troops
Dressed as if life were a continuous parade,
Thomas Woodrow Wilson, wreath in hand,
Stared at the sentinel crosses painted white
At Suresnes, in France. "I sent these lads
Over here to die.". . .A bugle pealed;
Then rifle-rattle and the wreath set down
To the bugle-moan of Taps
And sixty seconds of religious thought:
"Thank God, these others are dead!"
After the boredom of silence, Wilson's speech:
A patter of words that nobody understood
Since Wilson spoke in English when in France.
At the second volley of cheers
The open car's door opened and Wilson rode,
Accompanied by flowers, an army of flags and shrieks,
A line as far as sight's end of that crowd,
A guard of honor, the customary troops,
And a band that blared pure Sousa to the world.

What did he hold but a handful of ideals
Culled from his father's sermons, culled from knowledge
Of laws and governments,
And a brute knowledge transported to the heart—
So much suffering, so many dead—

"I sent these lads over here to die. Shall I—can I—ever speak
a word inconsistent with the assurances I gave them when I
came over?"

And a command of rhetoric, the South's sure magic,

With which to meet the Statesmen, devise the Peace?
Were his ideals, his very words, a sauce
Smothering the plate, obscuring knowledge
And ignorance in equal and in palatable measure?
(Words issue, repeat and circle words,
Circumnavigate the clutter and the matter of the heart,
Cross and criscross the filaments of brain
Until the initial shape that thought established
Is violated by another figure
Which is no figure, a shape of shapelessness,
The self involved in action and distraction.
How thus can men
Address when they address a nation's actions,
The actions and transactions of the world,
Unconfounded and without confusing
The visible, the semi-known, with the unknown,
Invisible, submerged leviathan? What man can speak
As if the boundaries, as if such lines—
There are no lines—between the known and semi-
        known and the unfathomed
Were clear, were marked, were common
                              knowledge, not
Common and uncommon ignorance?

"Everything is persistently impersonal. I am administering a
great office but I do not seem to be identified with it: it is not
me and I am not it. This impersonality of my life is a very odd
thing, and perhaps robs it of intensity as it certainly does of
pride and self-consciousness (and, maybe, of enjoyment) but it
at least prevents me from becoming a fool and thinking myself
It!"

Did It alone speak? Did Wilson and It interchange
With and without each other's recognition?
Such as they are, the facts, the little facts, are known:
A bed of questions; the questions have remained.
Yet is it cause for wonder
That Wilson said: "Tell me what is right?")

Would he not be
The prince of "peace without victory?"
For who but God could choose, had chosen
Those who would sit, would talk, would rule
Among the powers conjoined to forge
The Covenant and the Laws of Peace
Behind the painted gates and creaking fountains set
At the Sun King's palace at Versailles? He nearly
    smiled
And mumbled to himself his opening address. . .
The gray suede gloves that fitted the fat hands
Were locked across the belly's mount
Of Clemenceau, at Versailles, one eye closed
Entirely while a squat forefinger drummed
The gold-cased pocket-watch. One eye winked
As if a spasm of sunlight had dared to assault
The armor of calm made skin by habit and age.
Then that eye shut down. An aide poured forth
Liquid words that spurred both liquid hands
To a whirlpool of gestures. Clemenceau
Stopped drumming with the forefinger, smiled, said:
"Mon vieux, restez calme. Nous verrons."
        The finger drummed;
One eye opened to regard the watch:

Wilson again delayed by the barbarous crowds,
The dinner would be cold. He shut the watch
And wound it slowly, thinking: La France doit
    reigner! . . .
           After the final salute,
The final cannonade of cheers, the final halt,
The final screech of Sousa from the band,
Wilson sauntered to the palace at Versailles
To crown an unjust war
With a just peace and thereby crown his life
With the consummate coin of his unspotted prose.
The mirrors in the Hall of Mirrors blazed,
So minutely polished they disclosed
A perfect darkness spotted but not streaked
By what seemed candleflicks that blurred to smoke.
Seeing each mirror arrow to the next
A Wilson upon Wilson and each smaller,
The several Wilsons still as a parade
Of scissored, crayoned, paper figurines,
Each with a hand and arm upraised for help,
The last hand clutching darkness like a brother—
What did he see?
*"Which one am I? Which one is It?*
*Which one is Colonel House, my other self?*
Metternich, Pitt, Talleyrand, Sun King,
See, I have come
As once you came, the last just men of earth
As in the fable that the world becomes,
To Versailles in the name and cause of man!
See, I have come
Into your folly, your pride of mirrors, Reason's madness!

So that is Europe!
          Yet I cannot believe
A man could be, should be, so many men."

Lloyd George, Orlando, Wilson, Clemenceau
Conducted themselves with the practised, conspicuous
     tact
Of undertakers. They carved Europe into nation-legs
Without a head, without arms, without blood
Except for the blood of money for the next
War to keep the world safe for more wars,
More dividends. Item: Lloyd George:
"Please refresh my memory.
Is it Upper or Lower Silesia
We are giving away?" Such items formed the Peace,
What Wilson called the best that could be dredged
From a dirty past. The best? . . .
Late, too late, at false dawn,
The trousers bagged, the morning coat too large,
The President, a scarecrow's mockery,
On hands and knees crawled the carpeted floor
That was smothered with maps of Europe, Greek to
     him.
And begged:
"Tell me what is right and I will fight for it."
No aide knew what to reply
And the fighting itself had been done. When Lloyd
     George,
Confederate of chaos, tried to coax
Wilson to refuse the ruinous Peace,
The President was adamant, and nothing changed.

"I shall consent to nothing. The Senate must
Take its medicine." Did nothing change?
In his departure, in an open limousine,
The flowers stacked beside him were his wreath,
The band erupted into noise, the honor guard
And troops escorted him along the avenue lined
By the crowds that brought no flags, no shrieks,
No articles of joy. Silence while men stared
At Wilson riding in his funeral march.
No bugle sounded Taps, no rifle shot
Momentary pockmarks in the sky, no one addressed
Words to the living over the breathing corpse.
Thomas Woodrow Wilson, President,
Who in his boyhood, in his father's church,
Had steeled himself to speak to all mankind
In the name of God and man and the ideals
That he had thought worth striving, dying, for,
In this, his last event in France, was speechless, dumb,
Unmanned by machinations of his own
And of his fellow ministers.
                    In moments such as these,
The heart contracts, the blood stops, the mind balks,
And the imagination fumbles at the tears
That should have pearled the broken marble head
Of the Errant Knight, the shuttlecock of events.
But no one cried. No one shouted. No one moved
Until the funeral procession had become
A curl of smoke on the horizon, blown
By the hurrying wind from sight to no sure place.

Did he not ask the world to be unworldly once

As if the exercise of force, like any habit,
Men could start and stop by the command of will?
As if momentum
Were nothing in the intercourse of nations
And nothing in the traffickings of men?
As if the past
Did not obtrude to tangle present action,
As if there had been never yesterday?
As if the present time were God's renewed creation
And men the unvexed Adam setting forth
In a strange Eden much like El Dorado,
Its rivers, fields, woods, mountains, spread before us,
Its animals, fruit, fish and native men
Still to be known and named, but beckoning
Like a fresh green breast of the new world
Seen, not seen, in turning dreamfare
Before each woman, every man
Wakes to the nightmare of disjointed life
In which there is no history, no meaning,
Only the separated pieces of the news,
Only events without relation,
A static succession
Of places, names, dates, statements, and not actions
So often as almost actions that occur
With and without intention, a profuse confusion
Of happenings and only happenings?

"Tell me what is right and I will fight for it."

# XIX

## VETERANS

(Near the pond in Boston Common   1934)

It seemed as if their wars had never stopped:
Cuba, the Philippines, and Mexico.
Sometime during the first great war these two
Had been transferred, promoted, trained to teach
Young boys to shoot a gun straight and to crawl
And how, exactly how, to bayonet.
"It must have been a boring life," I said,
Handing each an apple. Nope. Grand fun.
A little colic, too, each now and then.
But mainly they remembered having fun.
And then a string of names I didn't know.
But women's names. They scouted me, returned
Their amble talk to war, to guarding banks,
To getting drunk. And then the names would flow.
This someone was alive, that someone dead,
Another was a cheat and officer.
How things had changed! How good their lives had been
When they were soldiers soldiering somewhere!
And here they were, civilians, much like men
Sitting on a park bench, taking the sun
In nineteen thirty-three or thirty-four.
By God! For all the notice they were given,
You'd think them dead, son, really, wouldn't you,
Or wandering around some soldier's heaven
Of barracks, drills, war games, and then the same

Done over, over through eternity?
While the silence, while the staring lasted
I sang a song my grandfather taught me
Until their staring fixed on me. They laughed
And picked me up and set me in a lap
Bone hard, bone brittle. All at once I knew,
As they played with me, tickled me, and sang
War songs they knew, that these two veterans
Were like a pigeoned statue turning green.
Did men turn green? I thought about that. Then
The three of us had wobble pudding which,
They let me know, was gunpowder and taste
Supplied by something else. How much they knew!
I didn't guess it then but later guessed
How useless knowledge is when you feel cold,
Not ordinary cold but the first chill
Down in the guts that lets you know you, too,
Have come as far as any man can come.
And so we sang. We sang the whole way home.
The songs were mixed with stories: long ago
Became right now until I seemed to see
Horses and dust, tall sugar cane, and men
Bitten and sick, and jungles all around.
I didn't see it then but later on
When I was maybe twelve and very wise
In a night dream I saw those two again
Clambering and killing for plain fun.
Waking, I knew what I should not have known
About the tiredness of two old men
Who, for an hour, much to their surprise,
For a small child became two little boys

As they had been when younger and would be
Once they entered training camp in heaven
Where everything would work by a routine
They knew by heart and had forever known.
And so I swore that they were innocent,
As innocent as I was when thirteen,
No matter what they'd seen or sung or done
When they enlarged the booty of these States,
The span of empire and appetite.

I pray to see those two good men again
The way I see them now: their eyes alive
With laughter, their two tongues at once at work
On stories, epithets, while their jaws grind
The plugs that stain their teeth a yellow brown,
And every while a zany song gets flung
To singe the sun and burn the coasting stars
In sheer defiance of propriety
And of the gods that, watching, maybe wink
And listen, smoothing their neat uniforms.

# XX

## PRAYER

(May, 1937    A minister speaks)

Here lies John D., depleted. How the times
Have changed since he would give dozens of dimes
Away in fair exchange for what he stole
In paper frauds to win himself control
Of nothing more substantial than mere oil!
He wrestled riches from such little crimes
And then returned by giving, no, not all,
Out of the ooze-black goodness of his soul
That he became a Christian parable
For folks like you and me to ponder well
Before we scoot to heaven or to hell
In cars and trucks moved by the grace of oil.

# XXI

## A PROFESSOR

A proper cane. A proper pair of gloves.
A suit to last ten years. A black briefcase.
A pearl stickpin. A regulated beard.
A proper photograph to be installed
In family albums to be made and sent
To relatives in that barbaric place,
America. The cane was smashed before him.
Because they fit, the gloves were commandeered.
A single photograph, but nothing else,
Was somehow smuggled out of Germany.
On my brother's wall, not long ago,
I saw that face again as if again
The foreknown had occurred: the shower stalls
With hundreds in each stall; the little minute
Before the wreckage was complete, the crumpled bodies
Removed and placed in dynamited ground.

What survives such knowledge? My firm bet
With nobody that this, my relative,
Purchased those nearly silver gloves, that walking stick,
That matchless suit at such a cost
As he could not afford in grandiose
Pride that he could not afford
To show those idiot Americans and those
Other idiots he lectured how a life
Was lived and should be lived if one lived in
The nineteenth century and carried on

Those manners and those customs surely
Because there had been Goethe, Beethoven and Heine
To prove the knack bravado
Could be accomplished and was worth the price,
Even the price of marching, head erect
And shoulders straight, at eighty, to the showers
That could not humble him, not any more.

# XXII

## EPITAPH: Hiroshima and Nagasaki

Fire, ash, smoke too thick for any breath.
Without a trace or warning or a care,
Mankind can be removed whole as a tooth
And leave what else remains of what is earth
Nothing or, if not nothing, nothing known.
And yet what else remains must persevere.
And does. Only by madness strong as death.
Unregenerate as they always are,
In that full madness men emerge once more
So to begin again what must be done
As if that had been done and done before
As often as the coming of the sun.

CODA

# FLOWER AND STREAM

Rocks, pebbles, irregular tufts of grass
On a level land that stretches past sight's end.
No trees. No birds. No motion. Not a sound.
There used to be a house where, once, a stream
Whistled against pale stone and disappeared
Into a steaming waterhole. Right there
Where water steamed should be by all the odds
The definition of a wilderness.
In that parched place
A sort of flower grows ragged and wild,
Its full height a few inches from clay ground,
The color of its petals a weak white.
More than years ago,
I thought the flower had to stand for—what?
No wiser, now I know
It grows because growing is what it does.
It does not choose its place. It does not choose
Its life, which it is helpless to refuse.
So, like a pilgrim, I return and stare
At such persistence in such emptiness
That somehow I grow nearly reconciled
Not with what I am supposed to be
But with what I am, all I cannot claim
Much blame or credit for. Have I become,
In any way,
A ragged flower (in a former place)
That blossoms beyond reason in the glare
Of summer that does not endure
Early August ice?

I cannot say.
But all the rest of what others call me
Is as the water is, a backward dream
A wayfarer would seize
If it were there—
No matter what the distance or lost roads—
White water rainbowing the ford
Before it tumbled underground with a surged hiss
That seemed to sound
A whistle like the beckoning of time.